The

Power

Of

Words

BY

ABU TAHER

1

Table of Contents

Disclaimer

The information contained in this eBook is for general informational purposes only. While we have attempted to provide accurate and up-to-date information, the content of this eBook may not be comprehensive, complete, or free from errors.

The author and publisher make no representations or warranties of any kind, express or implied, about the completeness, accuracy, reliability, suitability, or availability with respect to the information, products, services, or related graphics contained in this eBook for any purpose. Any reliance you place on such information is therefore strictly at your own risk.

In no event will the author or publisher be liable for any loss or damage including without limitation, indirect or consequential loss or damage, or any loss or damage whatsoever arising from loss of data or profits arising out of, or in connection with, the use of this eBook.

Introduction:

Words are the fundamental building blocks of communication. They help us express our thoughts, feelings, and ideas with others. Language is what sets us apart from all other species, and it is what makes us unique as human beings. We use words to connect with one another, to form relationships, to learn, to persuade, and to influence. The power of words is undeniable, and it is something that we often take for granted.

In this eBook, we will explore the incredible power of words and their impact on our lives. We will examine how language shapes our thoughts, emotions, and behavior. We will delve into the psychology and evolution of language, the art of persuasion, and the language of leadership. We will also examine the role of language in conflict resolution, relationships, success, and the future of communication.

The power of words can be used for good or evil. Words can inspire and motivate us to be our best selves, or they can be used to manipulate and harm others. Our words have the power to create and to destroy, to bring people together or tear them apart. They can be used to heal or to hurt, to empower or to disempower.

The words we use can have a profound impact on our mental and emotional well-being. Positive words have been shown to reduce stress levels, increase feelings of happiness and contentment, and improve our overall health. Negative words, on the other hand, can lead to feelings of anxiety, depression, and low self-esteem.

In a world where communication is more important than ever, it is essential that we understand the power of our words. We must use language mindfully, with the intention of building connections and promoting positivity. We must also learn to recognize the harmful effects of negative language and strive to eliminate it from our lives.

This eBook is designed to help you harness the power of words in a positive and effective way. It is a guide to using language to create meaningful connections, inspire others, and achieve your goals. Whether you are a business professional, a student, a parent, or simply someone looking to improve your communication skills, this eBook is for you.

So, let us explore the fascinating world of language together and learn how we can use the power of words to make a positive impact on our lives and the lives of those around us.

The Psychology of Language

Language is not just a means of communication; it is a complex cognitive process that involves various mental abilities. The psychology of language explores how our minds process and produce language, and how language affects our thoughts and behavior.

One of the most fascinating aspects of the psychology of language is the way in which we acquire language. Babies are born with the ability to recognize the sounds of all languages, but they eventually focus on the sounds of the language they hear most frequently. This process is called language acquisition, and it is a remarkable feat of cognitive development.

As we grow older, our understanding of language becomes more complex. We learn not only to produce words, but also to understand the meaning behind them. We learn the rules of grammar and syntax, and we develop the ability to use language to convey abstract concepts and ideas.

The psychology of language also explores how language affects our thoughts and behavior. For example, research has shown that the language we use can affect our perception of the world around us. People who speak different languages may have different ways of thinking about time, space, and causality.

Language can also influence our emotions. The words we use to describe our experiences can shape the way we feel about them. For example, research has shown that people who use more positive language in their writing tend to have lower levels of depression and anxiety.

The psychology of language also examines the way in which language is processed in the brain. Studies have shown that language involves multiple regions of the brain, including the left hemisphere, which is responsible for language production and comprehension.

Finally, the psychology of language explores the relationship between language and culture. Language is not only a means of communication; it is also a reflection of the values, beliefs, and customs of a particular society. The language we use can reveal a great deal about our cultural background and our personal identity.

In conclusion, the psychology of language is a fascinating field that explores the way in which language shapes our thoughts, emotions, and behavior. It is a reminder of the incredible power of words and the importance of using language mindfully and intentionally. By understanding the psychology of language, we can become more effective communicators and gain a deeper appreciation for the complex cognitive process that underlies this essential human skill.

The Evolution of Language

Language is a defining feature of our species, and it has played a crucial role in our evolution. The evolution of language is a complex and fascinating topic that has been the subject of much research and debate.

Scientists believe that language evolved gradually over a long period of time, and that it emerged as a result of changes in our brain structure and function. The development of language was likely driven by the need for social communication and coordination, as well as the ability to convey complex ideas and concepts.

One of the key features of language is its ability to convey abstract concepts and ideas. This ability to communicate in abstract terms is thought to be a crucial factor in the development of human culture and technology.

The evolution of language is closely linked to the evolution of the brain. Studies have shown that language processing involves multiple regions of the brain, including the Broca's and Wernicke's areas. These regions are thought to have evolved in response to the demands of language processing, and they are unique to the human brain.

Another important factor in the evolution of language is socialization. Language is primarily learned through social interaction, and it is shaped by the cultural and linguistic environment in which it is learned. This means that the evolution of language is also shaped by social and cultural factors.

The evolution of language has been the subject of much debate among linguists and anthropologists. Some researchers believe that language evolved gradually, while others argue that it emerged suddenly in response to a specific need or event.

Regardless of how language evolved, it is clear that it has had a profound impact on human society. Language has allowed us to communicate complex ideas, share knowledge and information, and form complex social structures.

In conclusion, the evolution of language is a complex and fascinating topic that has played a crucial role in human evolution. It has allowed us to communicate, cooperate, and create, and it continues to shape our lives in countless ways. By understanding the evolution of language, we can gain a deeper appreciation for the power and complexity of this essential human skill.

The Anatomy of Speech

The ability to speak is a defining characteristic of human beings, and it is made possible by the complex anatomy of our vocal system. The anatomy of speech involves a number of interconnected organs and muscles that work together to produce the sounds of human language.

At the most basic level, speech is produced by the movement of air through the vocal tract. This movement is controlled by the respiratory system, which includes the lungs, the diaphragm, and the intercostal muscles. When we inhale, air is drawn into the lungs, and when we exhale, air is pushed out of the lungs and through the vocal tract.

The vocal tract consists of several organs, including the larynx, the pharynx, and the oral and nasal cavities. The larynx, or voice box, contains the vocal cords, which are stretched across the opening of the larynx. When air passes through the vocal cords, they vibrate, producing sound.

The pharynx, which is located behind the mouth and nose, plays an important role in shaping the sounds produced by the vocal cords. The oral and nasal cavities also contribute to the shaping of sound, as the tongue, lips, and other articulators modify the flow of air as it passes through the mouth and nose.

The process of speech production is complex and involves the coordinated movement of many muscles. The muscles of the larynx control the opening and closing of the vocal cords, while the muscles of the tongue, lips, and jaw shape the sounds produced by the vocal cords.

The anatomy of speech also includes the auditory system, which is responsible for processing the sounds produced by the vocal system. When we speak, we not only produce sound, but we also listen to the sounds we produce in order to adjust our speech and make sure we are being understood.

In conclusion, the anatomy of speech is a complex and fascinating topic that highlights the incredible complexity of human language. By understanding the anatomy of speech, we can gain a deeper appreciation for the incredible skill required to produce the sounds of human language.

The Power of Positive Words

Words have a powerful impact on our emotions, attitudes, and behaviors. When we use positive words, we can create a positive and uplifting environment that can have a profound effect on our mental health and well-being.

Research has shown that using positive words and phrases can have a number of benefits, including reducing stress and anxiety, improving relationships, and increasing self-esteem. Positive words can help us to focus on the good in our lives and to develop a more optimistic outlook.

Positive words can also be used to motivate and inspire others. When we use words of encouragement and support, we can help others to achieve their goals and to feel more confident in their abilities. This can have a ripple effect, as the positivity we spread can inspire others to do the same.

One of the most powerful aspects of positive words is their ability to shape our perceptions of ourselves and others. When we use positive words to describe ourselves and others, we can create a positive self-image and promote a positive attitude towards others.

Positive words can also be used to counteract negative self-talk and negative thought patterns. By replacing negative words and phrases with positive ones, we can change our mindset and develop a more positive and resilient outlook.

In addition to their impact on our mental health and well-being, positive words can also have a physical impact on our bodies. Studies have shown that using positive words can lower blood pressure, reduce inflammation, and boost the immune system.

In conclusion, the power of positive words cannot be overstated. By using positive words and phrases, we can create a more positive and uplifting environment that can have a profound impact on our mental and physical health. We can also use positive words to motivate and inspire others and to promote a more positive attitude towards ourselves and those around us.

The Harmful Effects of Negative Words

Just as positive words can have a powerful impact on our emotions and well-being, negative words can have a detrimental effect on our mental health, relationships, and self-esteem. The words we use have the power to hurt, harm, and even destroy.

Negative words can create a toxic environment that can erode our self-confidence and self-worth. When we are subjected to negative words and criticism, we can start to believe that we are not good enough or that we are somehow flawed or defective.

Negative words can also damage our relationships with others. When we use hurtful or derogatory language, we can cause pain and resentment, leading to a breakdown in communication and trust.

In addition to their impact on our mental and emotional well-being, negative words can also have a physical impact on our bodies. Studies have shown that exposure to negative words and stress can increase blood pressure, reduce immune function, and contribute to chronic health problems such as heart disease and diabetes.

Negative words can also contribute to a cycle of self-destructive behavior. When we internalize negative messages, we may turn to unhealthy coping mechanisms such as substance abuse, self-harm, or disordered eating.

In conclusion, the harmful effects of negative words cannot be underestimated. The words we use have a powerful impact on our mental and physical well-being, as well as our relationships with others. It is important to be mindful of the language we use and to choose our words carefully, always striving to promote positivity and kindness towards ourselves and others.

The Importance of Listening

While the words we use have a powerful impact on our lives, it is equally important to recognize the power of listening. Listening is an essential skill that allows us to connect with others, build relationships, and gain a deeper understanding of the world around us.

When we truly listen to others, we are able to connect with them on a deeper level, fostering empathy, compassion, and understanding. We are also able to learn from their experiences and perspectives, broadening our own understanding of the world and our place in it.

Listening is also an important aspect of effective communication. When we listen attentively to others, we are better able to understand their needs, desires, and concerns, and to respond in a way that is respectful and helpful.

In addition, listening can also have a positive impact on our mental health and well-being. By being present in the moment and actively listening to others, we can cultivate a sense of mindfulness and reduce stress and anxiety.

Unfortunately, in our fast-paced and often distracted world, listening has become a lost art. Many of us are more focused on what we want to say or do next, rather than truly listening to what others are saying. This can lead to misunderstandings, miscommunications, and even conflict.

To become better listeners, it is important to practice active listening. This means being fully present in the moment, paying attention to both verbal and nonverbal cues, and asking clarifying questions to ensure that we fully understand what is being said.

It is also important to be aware of our own biases and assumptions, and to approach conversations with an open mind and a willingness to learn and grow. By doing so, we can create a more inclusive and empathetic world, one where listening is valued as much as speaking.

In conclusion, listening is an essential skill that allows us to connect with others, build relationships, and gain a deeper understanding of the world around us. By practicing active listening and approaching conversations with an open mind and a willingness to learn, we can cultivate empathy, reduce stress, and create a more inclusive and compassionate world.

The Art of Persuasion

Whether we realize it or not, we are constantly trying to persuade others to our point of view. Whether it is convincing a coworker to support a new project or persuading a friend to try a new restaurant, the ability to persuade is an important skill in our personal and professional lives.

The art of persuasion is not about manipulation or coercion, but rather about presenting our ideas and opinions in a way that is compelling and convincing. To do so effectively, it is important to understand the psychology behind persuasion.

One of the most important elements of persuasion is establishing credibility. This means presenting ourselves as knowledgeable, trustworthy, and reliable. When we are seen as credible, others are more likely to trust and believe in our ideas.

Another important aspect of persuasion is building rapport. This means establishing a connection with the person or people we are trying to persuade. By showing genuine interest in their perspectives and concerns, we can build trust and establish a foundation for open and honest communication.

In addition, it is important to understand the needs and motivations of the person or people we are trying to persuade. By tailoring our arguments to their specific interests and concerns, we can create a more compelling case for our ideas.

To be truly effective in persuasion, it is also important to be able to present our ideas in a clear, concise, and compelling manner. This means being able to communicate our ideas in a way that is easy to understand and that resonates with our audience.

Finally, it is important to be open to feedback and to be willing to adjust our approach as needed. Persuasion is not a one-size-fits-all process, and what works with one person may not work with another.

In conclusion, the art of persuasion is an important skill in our personal and professional lives. By establishing credibility, building rapport, understanding the needs and motivations of our audience, and communicating our ideas effectively, we can create more compelling arguments and achieve our goals. By being open to feedback and adjusting our approach as needed, we can become more effective persuaders and build stronger, more meaningful relationships with others.

The Language of Leadership

Leadership is about more than just telling people what to do. It is about inspiring and motivating others to achieve a shared vision or goal. One of the most important tools of a great leader is the language they use.

The language of leadership is about more than just choosing the right words. It is about communicating in a way that inspires confidence, trust, and loyalty in those who follow us. Great leaders use language to create a sense of purpose, to motivate and inspire, and to build a strong sense of team and community.

One of the most important elements of the language of leadership is clarity. Great leaders communicate their vision and goals in a way that is clear, concise, and easy to understand. They are able to articulate complex ideas and concepts in a way that is accessible to everyone, regardless of their background or experience.

In addition, great leaders use language to inspire and motivate their followers. They use language to create a sense of excitement and energy around their vision, and to create a shared sense of purpose and direction.

Another important element of the language of leadership is empathy. Great leaders are able to communicate in a way that shows they understand the concerns and perspectives of those they lead. They are able to create a sense of trust and safety that allows their followers to be vulnerable and to take risks.

Finally, great leaders use language to build a strong sense of team and community. They use language to create a sense of belonging and to foster a culture of collaboration and support. They are able to create an environment where everyone feels valued and included.

In conclusion, the language of leadership is a powerful tool that great leaders use to inspire, motivate, and build strong teams. By communicating with clarity, empathy, and a strong sense of purpose, leaders can create a shared vision and inspire their followers to achieve great things. By using language to build a sense of community and collaboration, leaders can create a culture of success that benefits everyone involved.

The Power of Storytelling

Human beings have been telling stories for thousands of years. From the cave paintings of our ancient ancestors to the novels and movies of today, storytelling is an essential part of our shared human experience. And while stories can be entertaining and enjoyable, they also have the power to inspire, motivate, and even change lives.

The power of storytelling lies in its ability to create a shared experience. When we tell stories, we connect with our audience on a deep and emotional level. We can use stories to convey complex ideas and concepts in a way that is easy to understand and remember. And we can use stories to inspire and motivate our audience to take action and make a difference in the world.

One of the most important elements of storytelling is authenticity. Great stories are not about creating a false sense of perfection or glossing over the difficult parts of life. They are about sharing our true selves and our real experiences, warts and all. When we share our authentic selves with others, we create a sense of vulnerability and connection that is essential to building strong relationships.

Another important element of storytelling is empathy. Great stories allow us to see the world through someone else's eyes. They allow us to experience the joys, sorrows, and struggles of others in a way that is both powerful and transformative. When we are able to empathize with others through storytelling, we create a sense of connection and understanding that is essential to building strong relationships.

In addition, great stories are often characterized by a strong sense of purpose. They have a clear and compelling message that inspires and motivates their audience to take action. Whether it is a call to action to support a cause, to change a behavior, or to pursue a dream, great stories have the power to move us and to make a difference in the world.

Finally, great stories are often characterized by their simplicity. They convey complex ideas and concepts in a way that is easy to understand and remember. They use vivid imagery and memorable characters to bring their message to life and to create a sense of emotional connection with their audience.

In conclusion, the power of storytelling is a truly remarkable thing. By sharing our authentic selves, empathizing with others, and conveying a clear sense of purpose, we can use stories to inspire, motivate, and even change the world. Whether we are sharing our own personal stories or using stories to convey a message or idea, the power of storytelling is an essential tool in our personal and professional lives.

The Role of Language in Conflict Resolution

Conflict is a natural part of human relationships. However, if left unresolved, conflicts can escalate and cause serious harm to individuals, organizations, and even entire societies. That is why conflict resolution is such an important skill, and language plays a critical role in the resolution process.

Language can either escalate or de-escalate a conflict. When individuals use inflammatory language or make personal attacks, conflicts can quickly become heated and emotional. However, when individuals use language that is respectful, empathetic, and solution-focused, conflicts can be resolved more effectively.

One of the most important aspects of language in conflict resolution is active listening. When we listen actively, we show the other person that we value their perspective and that we are willing to work towards a solution that meets both of our needs. Active listening involves paying close attention to what the other person is saying, clarifying our understanding of their perspective, and reflecting back what we have heard to ensure that we have understood correctly.

In addition, language can be used to reframe the conflict in a more positive light. By focusing on shared interests and goals, rather than the differences and disagreements, individuals can find common ground and work towards a mutually beneficial resolution. Reframing can involve asking open-ended questions, exploring the underlying needs and interests, and brainstorming creative solutions that meet both parties' needs.

Another important aspect of language in conflict resolution is the use of "I" statements instead of "you" statements. "You" statements can come across as accusatory and can put the other person on the defensive, making the conflict more difficult to resolve. In contrast, "I" statements focus on our own feelings and needs, and can help the other person to understand our perspective in a non-confrontational way.

Finally, language can be used to express empathy and understanding. When we acknowledge the other person's feelings and needs, and show that we are willing to work towards a solution that meets both parties' needs, we create a sense of trust and mutual respect that is essential for effective conflict resolution.

In conclusion, language plays a critical role in conflict resolution. By using active listening, reframing, "I" statements, and expressions of empathy and understanding, individuals can de-escalate conflicts, find common ground, and work towards mutually beneficial solutions. Conflict resolution is an essential skill in our personal and professional lives, and mastering the language of conflict resolution can make all the difference in our ability to resolve conflicts effectively.

The Language of Love and Relationships

Language plays a vital role in how we communicate our emotions and feelings in our relationships. The words we use can either build intimacy and trust or create distance and mistrust. Therefore, understanding the language of love and relationships is crucial for maintaining healthy and fulfilling relationships.

One important aspect of the language of love is expressing gratitude and appreciation. When we express gratitude, we communicate to our partner that we value and appreciate them. Saying "thank you" for small gestures and acts of kindness can go a long way in building a stronger emotional connection and creating a sense of mutual support and care.

Another essential aspect of the language of love is expressing affection and intimacy. Words of affection, such as "I love you," "I adore you," and "You mean everything to me," are essential for building emotional intimacy and deepening our connections with our partners. Moreover, physical affection, such as holding hands, hugging, and kissing, can also play a critical role in creating a sense of closeness and intimacy.

Effective communication is also essential in maintaining healthy relationships. Listening actively, being present, and validating our partner's feelings are all crucial skills for effective communication. In addition, using "I" statements, rather than "you" statements, can prevent defensiveness and make it easier for our partner to understand our perspective.

Another crucial aspect of the language of love is forgiveness. Being able to forgive our partner and communicate our willingness to move forward after a disagreement or conflict is critical for maintaining healthy relationships. Expressing remorse and taking responsibility for our actions can also play a vital role in rebuilding trust and intimacy.

Finally, the language of love involves setting boundaries and communicating our needs clearly. When we communicate our needs in a direct and respectful way, we create a sense of safety and trust in our relationships. Setting boundaries and saying "no" when necessary can also help us avoid resentment and maintain our individual identities within our relationships.

In conclusion, the language of love and relationships is vital for building healthy and fulfilling relationships. Expressing gratitude, affection, forgiveness, and effective communication are all essential skills for maintaining emotional intimacy and trust in our relationships. By understanding the language of love, we can deepen our connections with our partners and create more fulfilling and lasting relationships.

The Power of Affirmations

Affirmations are positive statements that we repeat to ourselves to change our thinking patterns and beliefs. The power of affirmations lies in their ability to change our mindset and help us cultivate positive thinking and self-belief. By repeating affirmations regularly, we can reprogram our subconscious mind and create new neural pathways that support positive self-talk and belief.

One of the benefits of affirmations is that they can boost our self-confidence and self-esteem. When we repeat affirmations such as "I am worthy," "I am enough," and "I am capable," we reinforce positive beliefs about ourselves and our abilities. This can help us overcome self-doubt and develop a more positive self-image.

Affirmations can also be used to create positive change in our lives. By repeating affirmations related to our goals, we can focus our attention and energy on the desired outcome. For example, if we want to improve our health, we can repeat affirmations such as "I am healthy and strong" or "My body is capable of healing itself." This can help us stay motivated and focused on our health goals.

In addition, affirmations can be used to cultivate a more positive and grateful mindset. By repeating affirmations of gratitude, such as "I am grateful for all the blessings in my life," we can shift our focus from what we lack to what we have. This can help us cultivate a more positive and grateful attitude towards life, which can in turn attract more positive experiences and opportunities.

Another benefit of affirmations is that they can help us manage stress and anxiety. When we repeat affirmations that promote calm and relaxation, such as "I am calm and peaceful," we activate the parasympathetic nervous system, which helps us relax and reduce stress. This can be particularly helpful during times of high stress or anxiety.

To get the most out of affirmations, it's essential to repeat them regularly and with intention. This means finding a quiet and comfortable space where you can repeat your affirmations without distraction. It also means choosing affirmations that resonate with you personally and that reflect the positive changes you want to make in your life.

In conclusion, affirmations are a powerful tool for changing our mindset and cultivating positive thinking and self-belief. By using affirmations regularly, we can boost our self-confidence, create positive change in our lives, cultivate gratitude and positivity, and manage stress and anxiety. The power of affirmations lies in their ability to shift our focus and attention towards positive beliefs and outcomes, which can ultimately help us live happier and more fulfilling lives.

The Language of Success

Success means different things to different people, but one thing that all successful people have in common is a positive mindset and the ability to communicate effectively. The language of success is characterized by confidence, clarity, and purpose. In this chapter, we will explore how the language of success can help us achieve our goals and reach our full potential.

One of the most important aspects of the language of success is confidence. Successful people believe in themselves and their abilities, and they communicate this belief through their language. Confident people use strong and assertive language, such as "I can" and "I will," and they avoid negative self-talk and self-doubt. By projecting confidence through their language, successful people inspire trust and respect from others, and they attract positive opportunities and experiences.

Another key aspect of the language of success is clarity. Successful people know what they want and they communicate their goals and expectations clearly and concisely. They use specific and measurable language, and they avoid vague or ambiguous terms. By communicating their goals clearly, successful people are able to focus their attention and energy on what matters most, and they are able to stay on track towards their objectives.

The language of success is also characterized by purpose. Successful people have a clear sense of their purpose in life, and they communicate this purpose through their language. They use language that is inspiring and motivational, and they avoid negative or defeatist language. By communicating their purpose and passion through their language, successful people are able to stay motivated and inspired, even in the face of challenges and setbacks.

Another important aspect of the language of success is the ability to communicate effectively with others. Successful people are skilled communicators who are able to connect with others and build strong relationships. They listen actively and empathetically, and they use language that is respectful and inclusive. By communicating effectively with others, successful people are able to build trust and collaboration, and they are able to achieve their goals more effectively.

In conclusion, the language of success is characterized by confidence, clarity, purpose, and effective communication. By using language that is positive, specific, and inspiring, we can cultivate a mindset of success and achieve our goals more effectively. Whether we are pursuing success in our personal or professional lives, the language we use can have a powerful impact on our ability to reach our full potential. By mastering the language of success, we can inspire ourselves and others to achieve great things and live fulfilling lives.

The Impact of Social Media on Language

Social media has revolutionized the way we communicate with each other, and it has had a profound impact on the way we use language. Social media platforms like Facebook, Twitter, and Instagram have given us new tools and new ways to express ourselves, but they have also changed the way we communicate in ways that are both positive and negative. In this chapter, we will explore the impact of social media on language, and how it has affected the way we communicate with each other.

One of the most significant impacts of social media on language has been the proliferation of new words and phrases. Social media has given us new ways to express ourselves, and it has created new terms and phrases that are unique to the online world. For example, we now have terms like "hashtag," "like," "follow," and "retweet," which have become part of the everyday language of social media users. Social media has also given rise to new forms of communication, such as emojis and memes, which have become an integral part of online communication.

Social media has also changed the way we use language in terms of brevity and efficiency. With the rise of platforms like Twitter, which limits messages to 280 characters, social media users have had to learn to communicate effectively in short, concise messages. This has led to the development of new language styles, such as "text-speak," which uses abbreviations and acronyms to convey meaning in fewer characters. While this can be an efficient way to communicate, it can also lead to misunderstandings and misinterpretations if the recipient is not familiar with the language.

Another impact of social media on language has been the rise of informal language and the erosion of formal language conventions. Social media platforms are informal spaces, and this informality has translated into the language that we use online. Social media users often use colloquial language, slang, and informal grammar, which can be seen as a departure from traditional grammar rules. While this informality can be seen as a positive development, it can also lead to the erosion of formal language conventions and a decline in writing and communication skills.

One of the most concerning impacts of social media on language is the rise of hate speech and cyberbullying. Social media has given rise to new forms of harassment and abuse, and this has led to an increase in hate speech and cyberbullying. Social media platforms have struggled to deal with these issues, and the language used in online interactions can often be hurtful, derogatory, and harmful.

In conclusion, social media has had a profound impact on the way we use language, and it has changed the way we communicate with each other. While social media has given us new ways to express ourselves and has made communication more efficient and accessible, it has also led to the proliferation of informal language, the erosion of formal language conventions, and the rise of hate speech and cyberbullying. As social media continues to evolve, it is important that we are mindful of the language we use online and that we strive to use language in a way that is respectful, inclusive, and empowering.

The Importance of Multilingualism

Language is one of the most powerful tools we have for communication, but it is also a tool that can divide us. In a world that is becoming increasingly globalized, multilingualism has become more important than ever before. In this chapter, we will explore the importance of multilingualism, both for individuals and for society as a whole.

One of the most obvious benefits of being multilingual is the ability to communicate with people from different parts of the world. In a globalized world, being able to speak multiple languages is an essential skill that can open doors to new opportunities and experiences. Multilingual individuals are better equipped to work in international businesses, to travel, and to communicate with people from different cultures. They are also more likely to be able to understand and appreciate different cultural perspectives, which can help to build bridges between different communities.

Another benefit of multilingualism is the cognitive benefits it provides. Studies have shown that learning multiple languages can improve cognitive function and enhance brain development. Multilingual individuals are often better at problem-solving, multitasking, and decision-making, and they may also have better memory and attention skills. This is because learning multiple languages requires the brain to constantly switch between different language systems, which can help to improve cognitive flexibility.

Multilingualism also has social benefits. In communities where multiple languages are spoken, being multilingual can help individuals to feel more connected and integrated into their communities. It can also help to preserve cultural heritage and identity, as language is often an important part of cultural identity. Being able to speak multiple languages can also help to break down barriers between different communities and promote social cohesion.

Finally, multilingualism is important for economic reasons. As the world becomes more globalized, businesses are looking for employees who are able to communicate with customers and clients from different parts of the world. Being multilingual can be a significant advantage in the job market, and it can also help to boost economic growth and trade.

In conclusion, multilingualism is becoming increasingly important in a globalized world. It provides individuals with a range of benefits, including the ability to communicate with people from different parts of the world, cognitive benefits, social benefits, and economic benefits. As a society, we need to value and promote multilingualism, both in terms of language education and in terms of supporting communities where multiple languages are spoken. By embracing multilingualism, we can build bridges between different communities, promote cultural understanding and social cohesion, and create a more connected and inclusive world.

The Language of Diversity and Inclusion

Language is a powerful tool that can be used to either include or exclude people. In this chapter, we will explore the importance of using inclusive language and the impact it can have on promoting diversity and inclusion.

The language we use can have a significant impact on how people feel about themselves and their place in society. When we use language that is inclusive, we create a more welcoming and accepting environment. On the other hand, when we use language that is exclusive, we can alienate and marginalize people. Therefore, it is important to be mindful of the language we use and how it may affect others.

Inclusive language involves using words and phrases that do not discriminate against people based on their gender, race, religion, sexual orientation, or any other characteristic. It means using gender-neutral language, avoiding stereotypes, and being respectful of people's identities and backgrounds. For example, instead of using "he" or "she," we can use "they" or "their" to refer to a person without assuming their gender. We can also avoid using words or phrases that are offensive or derogatory towards certain groups of people.

Inclusive language is important for promoting diversity and inclusion because it helps to create a sense of belonging and acceptance for everyone. When we use inclusive language, we send a message that everyone is valued and respected, regardless of their differences. This can help to build trust and strengthen relationships between different groups of people.

On the other hand, exclusive language can create barriers between people and make them feel marginalized or excluded. For example, using language that assumes everyone is heterosexual can make LGBTQ+ people feel invisible or excluded. Using language that is racist or xenophobic can create a hostile environment for people from different racial or ethnic backgrounds.

Inclusive language is not only important in our personal interactions but also in the workplace and in public spaces. In workplaces, using inclusive language can help to create a more diverse and inclusive culture, which can lead to higher levels of employee satisfaction, better teamwork, and increased productivity. In public spaces, using inclusive language can help to create a more welcoming and safe environment for everyone.

In conclusion, language plays a powerful role in promoting diversity and inclusion. Inclusive language helps to create a sense of belonging and acceptance for everyone, while exclusive language can create barriers and marginalize people. It is important to be mindful of the language we use and to make an effort to use inclusive language in all areas of our lives, from personal interactions to the workplace and public spaces. By using inclusive language, we can create a more diverse and inclusive society where everyone feels valued and respected.

The Ethics of Language Use

Language is a powerful tool that can be used for good or for harm. The way we use language can have a significant impact on individuals and society as a whole. In this chapter, we will explore the ethics of language use and the responsibility that comes with using words.

One of the key ethical considerations when it comes to language use is honesty. We have a responsibility to use language truthfully and to not deceive others through our words. This means avoiding lies, exaggerations, and misrepresentations. Honesty is essential for building trust in relationships and in society as a whole. When we use language dishonestly, we can damage relationships and create a culture of distrust.

Another ethical consideration when it comes to language use is respect. We have a responsibility to use language that is respectful of others and their identities. This means avoiding derogatory language, slurs, and offensive jokes. It also means being respectful of people's pronouns and using language that is gender-inclusive. Respectful language is essential for creating an inclusive and welcoming environment for everyone.

Another ethical consideration when it comes to language use is the impact our words may have on others. We have a responsibility to use language that does not harm others, whether intentionally or unintentionally. This means avoiding language that is racist, sexist, homophobic, ableist, or discriminatory in any way. We also have a responsibility to be aware of the power dynamics in our language use and to avoid language that reinforces or perpetuates inequalities.

Another ethical consideration when it comes to language use is the responsibility we have as communicators. We have a responsibility to ensure that our words are clear and that our message is accurately conveyed. This means avoiding vague or ambiguous language and being mindful of our audience and their understanding of the language we use. We also have a responsibility to listen actively and to be open to feedback about our language use.

In conclusion, the ethics of language use are an essential consideration in our communication with others. We have a responsibility to use language truthfully, respectfully, and in a way that does not harm others. We also have a responsibility to be aware of the power dynamics in our language use and to avoid language that reinforces inequalities. By being mindful of the ethics of language use, we can create a more inclusive and respectful society where everyone's voices are heard and valued.

The Power of Silence

When we think about the power of words, we often focus on what we say and how we say it. However, the power of silence should not be overlooked. Silence can be just as powerful as words, and in some cases, even more so. In this chapter, we will explore the power of silence and its importance in communication.

One of the most significant benefits of silence is that it can help us to listen more effectively. When we are silent, we can give our full attention to the person speaking and truly hear what they are saying. This can help us to understand their perspective and build stronger relationships with them. Additionally, silence can help us to process information and reflect on what we have heard, leading to more thoughtful responses.

Another benefit of silence is that it can help to create a sense of calm and stillness in communication. In our fast-paced world, we are often rushing to say something, anything, in response to what someone has said. However, taking a moment of silence can allow us to slow down and be more intentional in our communication. This can create a more peaceful and respectful environment where everyone feels heard.

Silence can also be a powerful tool for expressing emotions. In some situations, words may not be sufficient to express the depth of our feelings. Silence can convey a sense of sadness, anger, or awe that words cannot. For example, a moment of silence during a memorial service can be a powerful way to honor those who have passed away.

Finally, silence can be a way to assert power in communication. By refusing to speak or respond, we can convey a sense of authority and control. This can be seen in negotiations or in situations where one person is trying to dominate the conversation. However, it is important to use silence responsibly and ethically, as silence can also be used to manipulate or intimidate others.

In conclusion, the power of silence should not be underestimated. It can help us to listen more effectively, create a sense of calm and stillness, express emotions, and assert power in communication. However, it is important to use silence responsibly and in a way that is respectful to others. By incorporating silence into our communication, we can create a more thoughtful, respectful, and effective way of interacting with others.

The Future of Language

Language has been an essential tool for communication for thousands of years, and it has continued to evolve and adapt to the changing needs of society. As we look towards the future, it is clear that language will play a crucial role in shaping our world. In this chapter, we will explore some of the ways in which language is likely to evolve and impact our future.

One of the most significant changes we can expect to see in the future of language is the increased use of technology. Advances in artificial intelligence and machine learning are already transforming the way we communicate, with virtual assistants and chatbots becoming more common. In the future, we may see even more sophisticated language processing technology that can translate languages in real-time and assist with complex communication tasks.

Another trend that is likely to shape the future of language is the continued globalization of our world. As people and cultures become increasingly interconnected, we can expect to see the development of new languages and dialects that blend elements of different cultures. Additionally, the use of English as a global language is likely to continue to grow, with more and more people around the world using it as a second language.

The growing importance of sustainability and environmentalism is also likely to impact the future of language. We may see the development of new words and phrases to describe environmentally friendly practices and technologies. Additionally, there may be a shift towards using more eco-friendly language in our everyday communication, such as replacing phrases like "throw away" with "recycle" or "compost."

The increasing diversity of our societies is also likely to have an impact on the future of language. As more people migrate and travel to different parts of the world, we can expect to see more multilingualism and a greater emphasis on cultural diversity. This may lead to the development of new languages and dialects that incorporate elements of different cultures, or to a greater appreciation for the unique features of existing languages.

Finally, we can expect to see continued efforts to improve communication and promote understanding across different cultures and languages. Initiatives like the Universal Declaration of Linguistic Rights and the UNESCO International Mother Language Day are important steps towards recognizing the value of linguistic diversity and promoting linguistic rights around the world.

In conclusion, the future of language is likely to be shaped by a range of factors, including technology, globalization, environmentalism, diversity, and cultural understanding. As we move forward, it is important to recognize the power of language and to work towards creating a more inclusive and communicative world. By embracing the potential of language to connect us, we can build a brighter future for all.

Additional Resources for Further Learning

Congratulations on completing "The Power of Words"! This eBook has provided you with an overview of the importance and impact of language in various aspects of our lives. If you are interested in diving deeper into any of the topics covered in this book or expanding your knowledge of language and communication, there are many additional resources available.

Books:

"Words That Change Minds" by Shelle Rose Charvet: This book explores the art of persuasion and how to use language to influence others.

"Nonviolent Communication: A Language of Life" by Marshall B. Rosenberg: This book is a guide to communicating in a compassionate and effective way, even in difficult situations.

"The Storytelling Animal: How Stories Make Us Human" by Jonathan Gottschall: This book delves into the power of storytelling and why we are so drawn to narratives.

"Crucial Conversations: Tools for Talking When Stakes Are High" by Kerry Patterson, Joseph Grenny, Ron McMillan, and Al Switzler: This book provides strategies for handling difficult conversations and resolving conflicts.

"The Language Instinct" by Steven Pinker: This book explores the innate ability of humans to acquire and use language.

Online Resources:

TED Talks: TED Talks are short, informative talks on a wide range of topics, including language and communication. Some recommended talks include "The Surprising Science of Happiness" by Dan Gilbert and "The Power of Vulnerability" by Brené Brown.

Coursera: Coursera offers free online courses on a variety of topics, including communication and language. Some courses to consider include "Introduction to Public Speaking" and "Introduction to Linguistics."

Linguistic Society of America: The Linguistic Society of America is an organization dedicated to the scientific study of language. Their website provides information on language research, news, and events.

Grammarly Blog: The Grammarly blog offers tips and insights on writing and communication. They cover topics such as grammar, style, and tone.

Duolingo: Duolingo is a language-learning app that offers free courses in over 40 languages. It is a fun and effective way to improve your language skills.

These are just a few of the many resources available for further learning about language and communication. By continuing to educate yourself and expand your knowledge, you can harness the power of words and use them to create positive change in your own life and the world around you.

Conclusion:

Language is one of the most powerful tools we possess. It allows us to connect with others, express our thoughts and emotions, and influence the world around us. Throughout this book, we have explored the various ways in which language can impact our lives, from the psychology of language to the art of persuasion, and from the harmful effects of negative words to the power of positive affirmations.

One of the key takeaways from this book is the importance of being mindful of our language use. We have seen that the words we choose can have a significant impact on ourselves and others, both positively and negatively. By choosing our words carefully, we can build stronger relationships, foster a more positive self-image, and achieve our goals more effectively.

Another important takeaway is the role of language in promoting diversity and inclusion. As our world becomes more interconnected, the ability to communicate effectively with people from different backgrounds and cultures is becoming increasingly important. By embracing multilingualism and using language in a way that is respectful and inclusive, we can help to create a more harmonious and accepting world.

Finally, it is worth reflecting on the potential of language to shape the future. From the evolution of language to the impact of social media, we have seen how language is constantly evolving and adapting to the changing needs of society. As we move into the future, it will be important to continue to harness the power of language in new and innovative ways, to help us tackle the challenges of our times and build a brighter future for all.

In conclusion, the power of words is vast and complex, but with careful consideration and mindfulness, we can use it to create positive change in our own lives and the lives of others. By understanding the psychology, anatomy, and cultural nuances of language, we can become more effective communicators and leaders, and use our words to shape a more harmonious, inclusive, and prosperous world.